D0456466

Phyllis
& Jim 1:6-
Many Best
Fogerbone

THOUGH
LIONS
ROAR

THE STORY OF HELEN ROSEVEARE
Missionary Doctor to the Congo

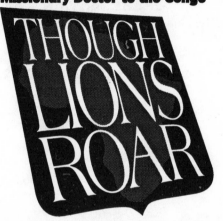

THOUGH LIONS ROAR

by Mary Beth Lagerborg

*Your enemy the devil prowls
around like a roaring lion
looking for someone to devour.*
1 Peter 5:8

CHRISTIAN • LITERATURE • CRUSADE
Fort Washington, Pennsylvania 19034

CHRISTIAN LITERATURE CRUSADE

U.S.A.
P.O. Box 1449, Fort Washington, PA 19034

GREAT BRITAIN
51 The Dean, Alresford, Hants., SO24 9BJ

AUSTRALIA
P.O. Box 91, Pennant Hills, N.S.W. 2120

NEW ZEALAND
P.O. Box 77, Ashhurst

ISBN 0-87508-663-2

First printing 1995

PRINTED IN THE UNITED STATES OF AMERICA

TABLE OF CONTENTS

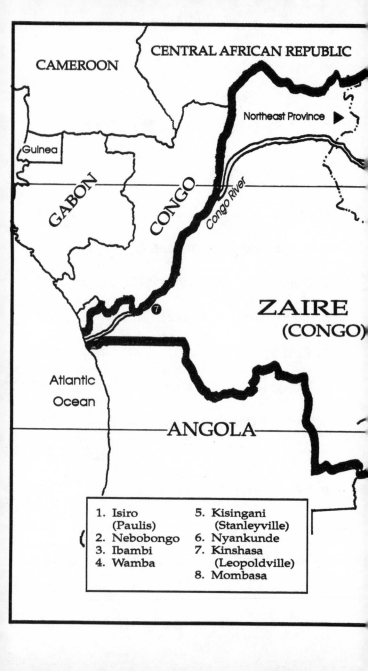

CAMEROON

CENTRAL AFRICAN REPUBLIC

Northeast Province ▶

Guinea

GABON

CONGO

Congo River

ZAIRE
(CONGO)

Atlantic
Ocean

ANGOLA

1. Isiro
   (Paulis)
2. Nebobongo
3. Ibambi
4. Wamba

5. Kisingani
   (Stanleyville)
6. Nyankunde
7. Kinshasa
   (Leopoldville)
8. Mombasa

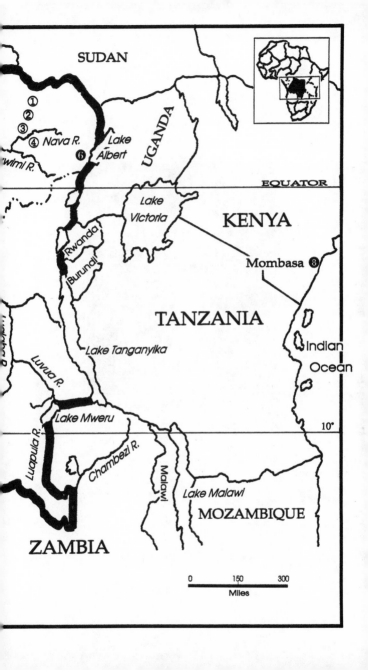

Dr. Helen Roseveare

1

SOMEBODY BIG ENOUGH

Helen Roseveare must have been bored. Or maybe the twelve-year-old was just annoyed with the number of rules at her boarding school in northern Wales. She meant well, but mischief was her shadow.

Helen planned a fire drill much more interesting than those devised by the Headmistress. "Let's pretend a fire broke out in the basement cloakroom," Helen whispered to the girls gathered around her. "Follow me. I'll show you how we could escape." They ordinarily followed Helen anywhere —she had the best ideas—until it meant trouble. But then they wouldn't own up to their part, and Helen would be the one confined to her room or a corner somewhere.

Helen climbed out one of the tall gymnasium windows, which were left open most days so the room wouldn't smell of active bodies. Carefully, she planted her footsteps on the slippery roof tiles, crouching as she crossed below the sewing room windows.

Then Helen wrapped her arms and legs

around a drain pipe and slid down it to the small, flat roof over the music room. The gray wool of her uniform skirt broke her speed. The girls smothered their giggles and were quite enjoying their escape until they were caught by the scowling Headmistress tapping on the music room window.

Helen wanted to lead the girls in good ways but couldn't quite figure out how. She wanted the girls to like her and look up to her. Meanwhile, something inside her had to be busy all the time.

Not attractive in any special way, Helen had light brown hair which resisted staying tucked in her braids. Her hazel eyes were framed with glasses. And until her older teens, Helen was nearly as thick across as she was tall. She never did get very tall. Yet the other girls were drawn to a sort of flame that ignited her, an intensity that made being around her always fun.

Her mind was as busy as her body. Helen devoured facts, knowledge. She especially liked science and math, with their logical patterns and methods of discovery. She was driven to get the highest grades, not to beat the other students but to know she could master the subjects.

Years before Helen's fire drill, in fact on

her eighth birthday, Helen decided what she wanted to do when she grew up. In Sunday school that day, Helen's teacher talked about faraway India. As she listened, Helen cut pictures of Indian children from magazines and pasted them in her Missionary Prayer Book. "When I grow up," Helen said to herself, "I'm going to tell other girls and boys about the Lord Jesus."

God seemed to be planting a first row of seeds in a little girl for whom He had a purpose. But it would be several years before Helen knew Jesus Christ well enough to introduce anyone else to Him, let alone travel to a faraway land.

Helen's father was a school inspector. Her parents took the family on long camping adventures through Europe for summer holidays. Helen adored and tagged after her older brother Bob. She also had three younger sisters—Diana and Frances, the youngest two, and next to herself, Jean —who loved to whisper in the dark of their bedroom at night, "Read to me, Peggy" (Helen's childhood nickname). Lying side by side under the blankets, by flashlight they devoured *Treasure Island*, *White Rabbit* and *Winnie the Pooh*, wrapped cozily in mystery, wonder and happiness.

The cloud of World War II hovered over Helen's life in her teenage days, especially when she traveled by train and bus from boarding school in Wales to her home in Kent, England. Her trips home took her through London, past many shabbily dressed people, filthy streets and gutted buildings. People hurried about their business with little chatter in the shops or on the streets. The German air blitz was under way. Air raid sirens warning people to take cover could shred the air at any time, day or night.

On one of Helen's bus trips, the sirens blared and two women leaped from the bus before it could come to a stop. They ran for shelter to the nearest home. As Helen stood in the aisle of the bus waiting her turn to get off, a bomb struck, shaking the bus and leaving the house next door a blazing mass. She watched in horror as the Civil Defense men tried to reach the screaming women.

As a teenager—especially as a teenager experiencing wartime—changes were taking place in Helen Roseveare. Within herself, Helen was not as perfect and as loved as she wanted to be. She kept talking in class and getting into trouble. On the outside, Helen hurt for the pitiful, tattered children who huddled around campfires in the alleys of London. Life seemed so useless.

The war went on and on. Helen grew conscious of her need for God. She knew she needed Someone Bigger than she was, than it all was; Someone who knew why things were happening and how they were significant. Helen longed for Someone who could cope with the whole world's needs as well as her own. Gradually she became aware that to reach this Someone she needed to be absolutely honest in her search. He must be big enough to hold the truth.

Helen was attending church, and there she went through the ritual of confirmation. She was searching for God, and confirmation seemed to be the way that people got close to Him. It brought no particular change to Helen's life then, but she realized later that God honored her serious search for Him. Behind the scenes He was planting more seeds in His purposes for her.

After boarding school, in 1944 Helen went to Cambridge University in England to study to be a doctor. Classes for medical students were being squeezed into two years to train doctors more quickly during wartime.

To give her a treat before school started, Helen's father met her in London and took her to a Gilbert and Sullivan opera. The next day she began the demanding life of a medical student.

Away from boarding school where she was so well known, in a place where she would have to prove herself in many new ways, Helen entered the tiny room that would be her home. As she filled the first lonely minutes putting her clothes into the dresser drawers, her eye caught a card stuck onto the mirror. It read "If you don't know anyone, and have nowhere to go after supper, come and have coffee in my room, number 12, at 8:00 p.m." and was signed "Dorothy." A lump blocked Helen's throat and her eyes blurred with tears. The day would be long, but now she had something to look forward to.

That evening Helen joined eight other students in Dorothy's small room. They sat on chairs, sofa, bed and floor, chatting about everything, with a kettle of coffee on the cozy fire in the grate. Helen felt welcomed and liked.

The next day Dorothy, or Dot, as she liked to be called, came for Helen early to walk with her to the dining hall for breakfast. Then she showed Helen around the campus and the town. They laughed and talked like old friends. Dot showed Helen the quickest route to the anatomy classrooms and which shops were the cheapest for buying books and stationery.

It was good that she had a friend, because the school days to follow were difficult for Helen. The anatomy dissection room, particularly, where the medical students poked and cut on dead carcasses, was a place of horror. She tried not to inhale the pungent smell of formalin, a chemical used to preserve the dead bodies. In front of her each day was a pale mass of something which had been living, which she had to pick and probe. Beside her on the bench was propped a greasy textbook showing diagrams of the organ that lay before her. Her fingers trembled and her mind numbed as a teacher often came up behind her, sorted out one strand of the mass and asked Helen to give the name, description and origin of what they were peering at.

At Cambridge there were many bright students, and studies were difficult for Helen. Her mind sometimes went blank in class for fear the teacher would ask her a question which would reveal her ignorance.

Outside of class Helen dealt with a different sort of problem. Helen was an Anglo-Catholic. On Sunday mornings she went faithfully to the formal Anglo-Catholic mass at Little St. Mary's Church. She liked to sit through the mass wrapped in a familiar sense of quiet reverence, of mystery and a holy peacefulness. But it was a very lonely worship; no one greeted her or spoke to her as she came and went.

On Sunday evenings, in contrast, she attended meetings of the Cambridge Women's Inter-Collegiate Christian Union (CWICCU) with Dot and her friends. These girls were quickly becoming Helen's friends. They were different, and Helen was impressed with them. They were happy, friendly, sincere, clean-mouthed and honest. They diligently studied the Bible, and —more impressive—they lived out what they believed.

To Helen the Bible was a book of dry history, grand stories and outdated myths. But impressed with her friends' love of it, she began to read the Bible with them and on her own.

Christmas vacation presented a new specter of loneliness for Helen. At home one of her sisters had the mumps—swollen glands in the throat, which were extremely painful. The virus could also settle in other organs and for a girl of Helen's age could be a serious illness. When she and her siblings had had chicken pox several years before, she had a particularly hard case. Later, when she had measles, her eyesight was permanently damaged. So for Helen's protection her parents decided that she should not come home.

Two friends from CWICCU invited her to their homes for two weeks. After that, they arranged for her to attend a holiday camp on the campus of a Bible college. She discovered when she arrived that it was a training camp for women who would be leaders the following summer at Christian camps.

During this holiday an inner battle raged in Helen. Slowly she had given up her Sunday visits to mass at Little St. Mary's, and she had become an avid student of the Bible. What she didn't know—and desperately wanted to—was how to take the Bible knowledge she loved and see it make a difference in the way she acted.

Helen knew that although she tried very hard to be perfectly good, she couldn't do it. She was a sinner before a holy God, and she was very lonely.

One night that fall, in her friend Sylvia's room, the Bible study group had sung the song "More about Jesus would I know. . . ." After the others left, Helen sat on the hearth rug and gazed at the twigs on the fire. She wanted so badly to know Jesus. As she sat there, the room glowed softly and Helen felt joy and wonder. She sat a long while, silently, holding the moment, then slipped away to her own room.

Now, at holiday camp, Helen again hungered to know Jesus in her heart. She joined in all the Bible studies and discussions. One night she curled up on the living room sofa with her Bible and a study guide on the book of Romans. She read the verses carefully and answered each study question. When she finally uncurled her cold, cramped legs and trudged up to bed, Helen passed two girls, fully dressed, on the stairs. "You're late," Helen said.

"You're early," they replied. It was 6:30 a.m., and they were reporting to help cook breakfast.

Finally, on the last evening, after arguing over a point of doctrine at dinner with some of the girls, Helen threw herself across her bed, feeling lonely and different from all the others. As she stared at the wall opposite her, a printed scroll on the wall caught her eye: "Be still and know that I am God" it read, from Psalm 46:10. And Helen, bright young woman of talk and action, was still. In the quiet room Helen received a great peace and knew that all the theories she had stored up were not only true and real and alive but they were personal and individual and hers. Jesus Christ, the only-begotten perfect Son of God, had died on the cross willingly for her, for Helen. He had risen from the dead and then ascended into heaven, and the sacrifice of Himself which He had made for sins covered all Helen's sins. The Holy Spirit would live in her heart as a Guide and a Comforter for her, if she believed these things were true.

Helen quit laboring to figure it all out perfectly in her head. She quit striving to be perfect in her own efforts. She accepted God's help. She accepted Him, the Someone Big Enough for her. Then she washed her face and went downstairs for the final evening's meeting with a glow about her which made the other girls ask, "What happened to you?"

2

SOMETHING BIG ENOUGH

Helen was completely caught up in the new love she experienced for Jesus Christ. Compelled to be active, Helen believed her new faith in God must also be active and show itself in her life.

Appalled at how little she still knew about the Bible, she now applied her love of learning to a thorough digging into Scripture. She tried to understand the meaning of each word, and how it related to her life. This became a pattern of studying the Bible which she would follow throughout her life.

In prayer meetings with other believers, Helen learned the sense of freedom which came when she honestly poured out her heart to God.

But how, Helen wondered, could she be certain she knew God's will? A friend explained these principles to her:

1. Through our daily Bible reading, God can speak to us through a passage, an example or a warning.

2. In daily prayer, as we talk a problem over with the Lord, as we wait quietly, He

can speak directly to our hearts.

3. We should seek the advice of Christian friends and people of greater experience who have had to make similar decisions in the past.

4. We should take into account the circumstances in which we find ourselves.

"Imagine one of these principles on each finger of your hand," her friend said. Then she moved her thumb to her fingers one after another. "Look for peace over a decision in each of these areas individually, and then in them all together. Let the peace of God umpire in your heart. If He is speaking, He will give you peace. If you don't have peace in these areas, the decision is probably not in line with His will for you." They were sound principles which Helen held onto for life.

In order to bring friends to faith in Jesus Christ—like her cricket team coach who was a member of the Communist student league—Helen invested many late-night hours with her friend, talking and studying the Bible. In the daytime they played cricket together.

All went well until Helen completed her grueling college classes and continued to the part of medical school that was taught on-the-job at West London Hospital. A wave of depression and doubt rolled over her during her first months at the hospital. She was afraid she couldn't measure up—and now she was working on live bodies, not dead ones!

Sadly, the enthusiasm of Helen's spiritual life seeped out. The closeness with other Christians she had enjoyed at college was sorely lacking at the hospital.

Helen asked permission to lead brief worship services in hospital wards, where there were many women patients within each large room. It was not that she really believed anyone in the wards would be led to believe, but it seemed like the thing a Christian medical student should do. So Helen passed through the wards with a harmonium, which was a tiny organ-like keyboard, and with song sheets. She handed out a song sheet at each bed where a person seemed able to participate, then played the harmonium with two fingers (not her strongest talent) and led singing— which was usually her solo. Then she prayed, read from the Bible, preached a short sermon, and moved on to the next ward of beds.

Every Sunday evening for three years Helen continued this practice out of a firm sense of duty. Then one evening she added the men's orthopedic ward, where sixteen mostly healthy fellows lay with legs or arms

bandaged and hoisted into the air as a re-
sult of motorcycle or similar accidents.

As she set up her harmonium, Helen
sensed this would not be the usual service. "What hymn should we sing first?"
she asked cheerfully. "Roll Out the Barrel"
was a tavern song suggested from the far
end of the room. Ignoring their request,
Helen gallantly attempted to sing number
seven on the song sheet: "Fight the Good
Fight"—a manly song, after all—while the
men at the end of the room began a rous-
ing chorus of "Roll Out the Barrel."

During the second verse of this discor-
dant "round" someone threw a boot, strik-
ing the harmonium. Helen continued with
the third verse, stalling so she had time to
pray what to do next. At the end of the verse
Helen heaved the boot back down to the
end of the ward. *I don't play cricket for
Cambridge for nothing!* she thought. The
men were so impressed that a girl could
throw so far and straight that they gave
her no further trouble, listened intently,
and after the service one young man even
gave his heart to Jesus Christ.

He was the first person to openly believe
in three years of those hospital services,
and Helen was both thankful and horrified. Why hadn't more people believed? Discouraged, she told herself that it was be-

cause her talk was one thing, but her actions didn't agree with what a Christian should be like.

More discouragement came in the same wards in front of the doctors who were her teachers. She felt crippled by a suffocating shyness and a fear that her work was inferior: fear of what the doctors thought.

Two factors fed into Helen's gloom. One was that she was exhausted from overwork —and when one's tired the world never seems as bright.

The other was her tendency to be too inward—to be caught up with her own thoughts and feelings too much. As it's been said, "A carrot can't grow if it is continually dug up to see how it is getting on." Finally, Helen gave over to God the failures she felt. He would have to fill the holes, to make up for what she felt she couldn't do. Helen realized God wanted her to think more about Him, and less about herself. *He* could see to it that Helen's faith grew!

During this dark time in Helen's life, a nurse friend invited her to see a movie after she got off duty one evening. They arrived late and had to stand in the back of the packed theater, craning their necks to see "Three Miles High," an account of missionary work in the Himalayan Mountains

on the border of Tibet. Helen stood en-
tranced by the magnificent beauty and
challenge of the film, as well as the amazing courage and determination it revealed.
Something inside Helen reached out to join
those people—to find a service for Jesus
Christ that would stretch her to her limits
and be big enough to require her all.

They stayed afterward so Helen could
talk to the man who had shot the film, Ma-
jor Leonard Moules. He gave Helen literature and invited her to the headquarters
of his mission agency: the Worldwide Evan-
gelization Crusade, or WEC. She went
home that night too excited to sleep. Helen
felt a new joy, a fresh challenge, a great
hunger for God, and decided to serve Him
at any cost—anywhere.

She visited WEC headquarters in London, and the next June, while she was still
a medical student at West London Hospital, began living there. Many young adults
stayed at headquarters while they prepared
for missionary service in other countries.
Lively talk around the dinner tables was
centered on the Lord, on issues of doctrine,
and on missionary strategies. They prayed
for revival, a rekindling of fervor in the
church, sometimes into the early morning.
They prayed for missionaries and govern-
ments and projects, and about persecu-

tions and triumphs from Colombia to the Philippines. Their lives radiated earnestness and warmth and truth, and Helen wanted to be one of them.

While she completed her studies and work at West London Hospital, Helen also cared for Edith Moules, sister-in-law to Leonard Moules, at WEC, for the final six weeks of Edith's life. Mrs. Moules had been WEC's first medical missionary in Africa, in the Belgian Congo and later along the west coast of Africa, working primarily with lepers. From her bed, Edith taught missionary candidate nurses and dictated letters to those still caring for lepers in Africa. Of course Helen had no idea then that she would not only *see* but herself *do* the work Edith had begun in the Belgian Congo. More seeds were being tucked into Helen's life.

As Helen completed her final exams and so became a doctor in the fall of 1950, she made the transition from a student living at WEC to a missionary candidate training at WEC.

This meant a shift from the sick room to the rest rooms, because Helen now had to help with the housework. And she had reached her mid-twenties never having performed a household chore.

Her first assignment was washing the

cement floor of the bathroom on the women candidates' floor. Helen took a bucket and brush and had at it. On her hands and knees, she scrubbed out the first toilet stall and began on the second. She could see muddy feet enter clean stall number one, the floor of which was still wet. When the feet left, Helen slipped back into the first stall and cleaned it again. As she did, feet appeared in still-wet stall number two. As this continued, the old sense of failure pricked at Helen, bringing tears to her eyes. She muttered in frustration. Elizabeth, Helen's supervisor, entered the rest room and watched quietly. She asked Helen why she was so upset, and when Helen explained she asked, "For whom are you scrubbing this floor, Helen?"

"Why, for you, of course."

Helen never forgot Elizabeth's answer: "No, my dear. If you are doing it for me, you may as well go home. You'll never satisfy me. You're doing it for the Lord, and He saw the first time you cleaned it. That is tomorrow's dirt." This experience helped Helen learn to do a job the best she could, then leave the results to God and move on to the next task.

From her assignment over the rest rooms, Helen moved eventually to the kitchen, but her stint with the cooking was brief and unsuccessful. Male missionary candidates teased her that her cooking was a means of getting sick patients on which to practice medicine.

The laundry seemed less threatening. Elizabeth demonstrated the process to her. It began with soaking the mountain of thirty-six sheets, pillowcases and towels, plus white overalls and the men's white shirts. Next the load was moved through the boiler, the rinse tub, then through the mangle to squeeze out the water (Watch your fingers!). It was all hung on the garden clotheslines to dry, then neatly folded and piled in the cupboards. Helen threw her own personal laundry into the vast pile to save time.

At about three in the afternoon on the first day, an agitated Elizabeth came to find Helen. "What have you done?"

Helen peered around, afraid perhaps she had set the house on fire. All the laundry dancing in the wind on the maze of clotheslines was green!—all except Helen's green socks, which were now boiled white and shrunk to the size of a child's. Elizabeth hadn't thought to tell Helen to separate the colors from the whites.

But Helen learned and settled into a happy routine. She was so ready, so eager to go to the mission field—but where? Every week missionaries on furlough poured in and out of the WEC headquarters, and all of them, from thirty countries, pleaded for more helpers—especially doctors. Daily Helen prayed for guidance.

One Tuesday in April 1951, Helen tore off the day's calendar page in the dining hall and read the text, puzzled. "Repair the house of the Lord" it read, from the book of II Chronicles in the Old Testament. What was this about? She stuffed the slip in her pocket and forgot it.

That week Helen received a letter from an old school friend, and enclosed was the same torn-off calendar page. She said the Lord urged her to send it to Helen. Amazed, Helen read carefully through the Scripture passage but could not see what the Lord was saying to her.

Then on Friday during morning prayers, the leader read the same verse from the same calendar slip. She explained how the Lord had burdened her, when she first read it, to pray especially for the Belgian Congo, WEC's oldest mission field, where more than 1,500 leprosy patients and over a quarter of a million Congolese looked to WEC for their medical care as well as for spiritual and educational help. "And yet," she said, "after thirty years of pioneer work and earnest prayer, we still have no doctor to offer them. Surely this lack is as a 'breach' in the wall of the church of God in Congo, and *He* needs us to be burdened to 'repair the house of the Lord.'"

Helen couldn't get away from the certainty of what this implied. Yet she wanted to go anywhere else. She was an evangelist, a preacher, a pioneer—and the Congo was an established work, a ministry to people who were already Christians. Surely God could better use her with people who had never heard about salvation through faith in Jesus Christ.

Sunday clinched it. As Helen cycled to church, she prayed earnestly that God would speak to her so certainly that she could not be mistaken. The pastor read the story of Balaam and his ass from the book of Numbers, chapter 22, and preached on verses 31 through 33. "Three times the Lord has clearly spoken to you," he said. "But you do not want to heed. You want something special and dramatic. Beware! He may not be patient for ever. Heed his voice in His thrice-repeated message and obey—and He will bless." So Helen was convinced. It was to be the Belgian Congo.

After six months' training at WEC, it was time for Helen and four other missionary candidates to be accepted into fulltime service with the mission. On that morning of

June 27th, the mission's quarterly staff meeting was in session in the library, and Helen was asked to take fifty coffee cups and saucers to the hall outside the library for them. The swinging door into the hall was stiff and heavy. Helen backed through the door, pressing slowly and carefully to balance the heavy tray. Once into the hall, she overheard the meeting. She couldn't hurry with the tray, nor could she close her ears, although she willed them closed when she realized they were discussing her!

Helen lowered the tray to the table and fled to the safety of the laundry room, her face crimson at the words she had heard: proud, always knowing better than others, unwilling to accept criticism and difficult to live with.

She picked up a basket laden with sixteen wet sheets, trudged up the stairs with them, and hung them on the clotheslines that crisscrossed the garden. The breeze refreshed her burning cheeks, and she was thankful to be able to hide for a while behind the billowing partitions of white.

Turning to get another load, Helen heard a twang. Spinning round, she saw the sheets she had soaked, boiled, rinsed and squeezed falling to the mud. Suddenly the tension broke, and it all seemed funny to Helen. With a belly laugh that erased the pain and worry of a few minutes earlier, she exclaimed, "Hallelujah!"

From the library windows above the garden, the forty missionaries and home staff members who were meeting saw the disaster. As they heard her laugh and exclamation, grins spread from face to face. And when they returned to their discussions, Helen was approved as a missionary with WEC. A sense of humor seemingly helped make up for what she lacked in other areas.

Later that day Helen was called into the staff meeting. They asked if she had any particular Scripture verses she wanted them to read, and she requested Isaiah 58:1–11, verses which had inspired her to want to serve the Lord as a missionary.

Standing before them, Helen's face turned scarlet and she trembled as the reader did not stop with the 11th verse, but read on through verse 12:

> *And those from among you will rebuild the ancient ruins; you will raise up the age-old foundations; and you will be called the repairer of the breach, the restorer of the streets in which to dwell.*

Helen felt God's hand upon her, propelling her into a special task in a foreign place. After asking her a few questions and giving her loving advice, the missionaries all shook hands with Helen, the newest member of WEC.

After a short holiday, Helen spent eight months in Belgium studying tropical medicine and learning French—the language spoken in the Congo, which was then a Belgian colony. Then for three months she raised support and purchased medical supplies, packed and said her good-byes to family and friends. On her final evening before sailing for Africa, February 13, 1953, Helen spoke to the WEC staff and thanked them for putting up with her the three-and-a-half years she had lived there. "So you should!" they replied merrily, in unison, catching her off guard.

Determined as she was to go, Helen was anxious, too. She worried about loneliness: she had great needs for friendship. Would she find good friends there? Language and communication also: languages had not been her strong suit in school, and her shyness made it difficult enough to communicate in English, let alone in French or Swahili. Doing without the luxuries of life and roughing it didn't bother her. But she shivered at the thought that she would have to carry heavy responsibilities and make crucial decisions without much experience.

Some months before she left for Africa,

Helen went camping in northern England and climbed up a mountainside to be alone with God. As she lay on the heather-covered hillside watching the clouds drift by, she tried to give herself—as much as she knew how—entirely to God and to His service. She thought of this hymn stanza:

> Stir me, oh! stir me, Lord, I care not how,
> But stir my heart in passion for the world:
> Stir me to *give*, to *go*, but most to *pray*:
> Stir till the blood-red banner be unfurled
> O'er lands that still in heathen darkness lie,
> O'er deserts where no cross is lifted high.

She glimpsed that a struggle lay ahead of her, and she prayed this prayer in all sincerity: "Please go on working in me until I really am transformed into the image of Your Son. Today I mean this, with every ounce of my being, but when You start doing it, and the stirring hurts, and I feel I can't take any more, maybe I'll cry out to You to stop. Please, when that happens, don't listen to my cry to stop, but just remember my vow today to be available to You, and just go on working away at me to make me like You want me to be."

Helen longed that the faith God put in her heart would always be living and active.

3

THEIR CHILD AT HOME

Helen's journey of 6,000 miles to Ibambi, Belgian Congo, took slightly more than five weeks from the day she sailed from London on the *Dunnotar Castle* in February 1953. On board ship for nearly three weeks, Helen studied Swahili and gathered with the other missionaries in deck chairs for Bible studies. Meanwhile, the *Dunnotar Castle* sliced its way through the Straits of Gibraltar to Genoa, Italy, then down the length of Italy and across the Mediterranean Sea to the Suez Canal. The days grew hotter and hotter as they passed Aden and skirted the east coast of Africa to the port at Mombasa, Kenya. Here Helen felt Africa's smothering welcome: unbearable heat, flies and thirst, and the noisy press of people in the streets.

She crossed Kenya by train, so excited that she couldn't eat or talk—barely even think. She rushed from one side of the train car to the other so she wouldn't miss anything out the windows on either side. At each station where the train stopped, she got out to stand on African soil, to read the name of the station, to feel, smell and see Africa.

Then by steamer she crossed huge Lake Victoria, larger than Lake Michigan of the Great Lakes. Another train carried her from Lake Victoria to Lake Albert, which straddles the border between Uganda and the Congo. So much water! The Belgian Congo, which is today called Zaire, is largely a huge rain forest drained by the Congo (or Zaire) River and its many tributaries—the second largest river in Africa.

Her last morning on the steamer, Helen stood at the railing from 4:00 a.m. onwards. In the warm, soft air, Helen watched the sun rise, bathing the mountain range to the west of the lake in golden red. The Congo! Helen was home.

Jack Scholes, the field leader of WEC, met Helen with the mission truck. After clearing all her baggage through customs, he drove her into the mountains on twisting hairpin curves. They descended the mountains on the far side into grasslands dotted with red buffaloes and antelope. Then they were swallowed into the Ituri Forest—miles and miles of jungle forest with a canopy of towering trees, rampant vines and dense undergrowth. Each night

of their journey they were warmly welcomed at a mission station to sleep.

Finally, they reached the last half-mile
to home. They drove down an avenue of
palm trees, through an arch made of flowers and a banner made of fabric which said
"Welcome to Ibambi." But the sound was
the best! The Africans, dressed in bright
print fabrics, were singing in Swahili to the
pulse of drums. The exuberant music was
like waves of welcome which rolled over
Helen. When they stepped out of the truck,
Jack and Helen were engulfed by the crowd
of Africans and missionaries. Pastor Ndugu
stepped forward, a tall, upright African
with a hint of gray in his receding hair. He
was the senior elder of the African church,
and would later become like Helen's African father. He gave a formal greeting: "We,
the church of Jesus Christ in Congo, and
we, her elders, welcome you, our child, into
our midst," he said solemnly. Then he
smiled, and it was as if the sun shone.

Helen's heart raced. What a privilege for
a young missionary to be "their child," one
of them.

The singing, the hand-shaking seemed
endless. At last Helen, overwhelmed,
slipped up onto a porch, or verandah, to
watch.

Before long Tamoma, Pastor Ndugu's

slight wife, came up beside her, her eyes shining and a dimple teasing her left cheek. Tamoma put her arm around Helen's shoulders. "I love you," she said, in Swahili, but Helen understood.

"But you don't know me," Helen laughed, amazed.

Tamoma explained she had prayed many years for a doctor for her people. When they heard that a medical student was interested, she had prayed Helen through her exams and preparations. She was certain Helen was God's special gift to them.

Ibambi would never be a strange place to Helen. She was already "their child," loved, and sung to in welcome. How could this not be home?

Early the next morning, clad in her white coat and with a cup of coffee in her hand, Helen was at work in her clinic. It had been converted from a mission office—a brick building with a cement floor, shuttered windows, and a verandah, where each morning a long, ragged line of Africans waited to see the new doctor. To work with, she had a camp stool, a table, some shelves, and a few medicines. Patients funneled in to her from the verandah. It teemed with crying babies, heat, the smell of vomit, people with oozing sores and everyone talking at once in a language Helen didn't understand. Helen's head swam. She had to consciously focus on what she was doing so she wouldn't faint.

At dusk, when the last patients drifted to their homes, Helen cleaned out the room, sorted the medicines that were left and made a list of the supplies she urgently needed. She was nearly too weary to walk and feared that she couldn't cope with the work. But of course she would give her best try. Each day Helen was at the job from early morning and was involved with paper work by kerosene lamp late at night. Jack Scholes couldn't help but notice both her drive and her obvious ability.

One evening during that first month, Jack drove Helen to an emergency in a village 12 miles off the main road in the jungle. As they lurched along the rutted roads, Jack talked to Helen as her supervisor and as a sort of missionary father. He talked about the mission, about ways he had experienced the Lord working, and about what success meant as a missionary: "If you think you have come to the mission field because you are a little better than others, or as the cream of your church, or because of your medical degree, or for the service you can render the African church, or even for the souls you may see saved, you will fail." He told her that the one thing the Lord cares about most for each of us is to make us more like Jesus. God was interested in Helen's relationship with Him. She must let Him take her and mold her as He willed. All the rest would take its rightful course. Helen listened respectfully, but it was a lesson she would have to learn in other ways.

At work in the clinic, Helen's old fear of failure reared its head often. As the only doctor for hundreds of miles around, she was expected to do many things that she'd never done before. One day a pygmy woman (pygmies were a people well under five feet tall) was brought to the clinic who had been in labor for several days and was very weak. Unless her baby was delivered by surgery, by Caesarean section, the woman would die. Helen had never performed surgery, not even in medical school—because, frankly, she didn't like the sight of blood.

By lantern light, without electricity, with a nurse who turned the pages of the medical book by her side, Helen attempted to deliver a healthy baby. She was petrified; she wasn't sure of what she was doing. And although she tried her best the baby died— and the mother died too, of infection, a few days later.

Helen was badly shaken as she walked home that night. What she had so feared had come true. She felt so guilty. She was a failure. She had had no business experimenting on an African.

Less than a week later, another woman was brought to the clinic who needed Helen to perform a Caesarean section in order to live. "I can't do it. I won't do it! It isn't right," Helen responded.

But of course she had to do it, because there was no one else. Fortunately, this time all went well, and both mother and baby thrived. It was a good thing, because Helen would have to deliver many babies by C-section in the years ahead.

One such delivery stood out. While Helen delivered a child one night by lantern light, the mother died. She left a two-year-old girl and the tiny premature infant, who would both go to the orphanage because they had no other family members to care for them. Helen and the nurses swaddled the baby in a blanket and prepared to place her in a box with hot-water bottles on either side to keep the wee baby warm. They were down to their last hot-water bottle, and it burst as a nurse poured boiling water into it, nearly scalding the nurse and leaving the baby without warmth for the chilly tropical night.

Helen walked over to the orphanage each noontime for the pleasure of talking to the

children and playing games and praying
with them. That day, as children gathered
round her sitting in the cool shade of a tree,
she told them about the tiny infant. "Please
pray that the Lord will help the nurses to
stay awake tonight so they can keep the
baby warm," Helen asked.

Ten-year-old Ruth had another idea, and
she prayed in the forthright manner of African children: "Please, Lord, send us a hot-
water bottle. Now God, it won't be any use
tomorrow, so please send it today. And
while you're at it, Lord, please send a dolly
so her sister will know Jesus loves her."
Helen couldn't help opening her eyes in
surprise as Ruth prayed—not believing
such a thing would really happen.

That afternoon a truck entered the village and left a parcel on Helen's verandah.
It was the first package she had received
from England in all the time she had been
in Africa. Villagers gathered around Helen
as she ceremoniously cut the string and
tore off the brown paper peppered with
stamps from the United Kingdom. Carefully, she untied each knot and folded the
paper. Inside she dug to packages of bandages, knit sweaters, soap—and a brand
new hot-water bottle.

Ruth stood watching from the front row.
"If God sent the hot-water bottle, He must

have sent the dolly!" she exclaimed. Ruth dove into the box with both brown arms and from the bottom pulled up a cloth doll. Ruth looked up at Helen with bright eyes. "May I go with you to give her the dolly to show her that Jesus really loves her?" Helen's eyes filled with tears.

She knew that the package must have been en route for five months. So five months ago, friends had sent a hot-water bottle to a missionary who lived on the equator and had tucked in a doll, in response to the future fervent prayer of an African child.

Time and again Helen was overwhelmed with the love that the Africans showed her. It wasn't as in England, where you got to know someone and then came to like them. Here in the Congo people loved her, then got to know her. And they liked this lady who worked so hard and was always ready and eager to help them. Sometimes when Helen got tired, she was impatient and spoke sharply. But she was immediately sorry and quick to ask for forgiveness, which the Africans warmly gave her.

Even for someone with Helen's capacity for work, the needs were overwhelming. She drove by jeep to the villages in the huge rain forest surrounding Ibambi, and saw clearly the need for a clinic at each village.

And in her mind's eye—as well as in her heart—she saw what her purpose was to be. She saw how she could "repair the walls."

She would train African Christians as nurse practitioners to staff these outlying clinics. She would train them to be nurse-evangelists, able to meet people's medical needs and to preach the gospel to them also. Her goal as teacher would be to enable each nursing student to pass the test to obtain a government assistant nurse diploma.

It was an encouragement to her when John Mangadima, a stocky young African, a student nurse at the Red Cross hospital in the northern part of the Belgian Congo, arrived and told Helen simply that God had sent him to work with her in the church medical service.

Then, shortly before Helen's first Christmas in the Congo, seven other student nurses joined her in Ibambi. The first students were ready. All they needed was a school.

4

FULL SPEED AHEAD

There was no doubt that Helen was a visionary. In her mind's eye she could see the natural outworking of plans she believed the Lord was giving to her as a repairer of walls. She saw a grand scheme of a large mission hospital with smaller clinics dotted throughout many miles of jungle. African nurse practitioners and midwives for the clinics would be trained at a nursing school at the mission head-quarters in Ibambi. But the mission leaders and the elders of the African churches in the area had another plan.

Seven miles to the north lay Nebobongo, the remnant of a large hospital begun by Edith Moules for leprosy patients. In the past few years the leprosarium had been moved to another location. Now left in Nebobongo were only a maternity hospital, where babies were delivered and midwives were trained to deliver them, and a home for the orphaned children of leprosy patients.

What had been a bustling village with

gardens and houses for the medical and field workers was becoming overgrown by the creeping green tendrils of the jungle. Nebobongo was now the domain of women and children. The forty children, ages infant to ten, were quite a sight as they sat at tables on the long orphanage verandah, in colorful cotton playsuits, singing grace before eating steaming bowls of rice, plantains and manioc root. The student midwives cared for the children, each with an infant tied on her back or a child on her hip.

Nebobongo was not Helen's first choice for the main hospital, but the choice was not hers to make. She was determined to make the best of it, to see her dream come true; and her first day there she was out with three workmen, crisscrossing the area a hundred times with a pencil, paper and a tape measure, making plans for rebuilding, then changing and remaking them.

Helen could see the needs and opportunities clearly. The problem was that she alone was equipped to take care of them all. Once the needed buildings were planned out, there were workmen for her to supervise. The orphans needed schooling, so she taught them. Then, of course, she taught the twenty nursing students—mostly sixteen- to twenty-year-olds—planning each night for the next day's classes. She managed the mission money for Nebobongo's food and supplies. She treated patients, performed operations, and when she could she visited outlying villages that needed medical care. In addition, she taught Bible lessons each morning.

Helen began her day at 5:30 a.m. with devotions and finished with paperwork in her office at 10:30 p.m. Often her sleep was interrupted by medical emergencies.

Each morning patients lined up on the hospital verandah—often 150 per day—with everything from malaria to crocodile bites. And when some had come 400 miles, how could she turn anyone away?

On the one hand, Helen had never been happier. In all ways Nebobongo was thriving. Once again there were neat houses and gardens for medical and village workers. Illnesses were treated and prevented. Nurses were learning. The children, if not excited about their studies, were happy. And Helen was responsible.

She had full opportunity to stretch all her talents, she had no head doctor to report to, and the Africans worked diligently and willingly by her side. But with the flow of pride she felt there was also a prick of conscience. Was all this to her own glory and not necessarily to God's? She was proud of her big family: her nurses, her workmen, her hospital, her vision. God still had to teach her that they were not hers, but His.

On the other hand, she often felt she was a failure. Her feverish pace cramped the time she spent alone with God, praying and reading the Bible. This time became a sliver in the routine, and stale. Helen became irritable with problems and interruptions and, worse, with the people around her.

One morning Helen held an eye clinic at 9:00 a.m. She readied her house, darkened the rooms, got out her instruments and waited. Patients trickled in—slowly enough that Helen had time for coffee breaks, and she didn't really want to spend her time over coffee. At the scheduled closing time for the eye clinic, Helen put things away and went over to the hospital to make her rounds.

Her house-helper came to tell her that a woman was waiting at the house to have her eyes tested. Annoyed, Helen asked where the woman was from. Since it was a village nearby, she snapped that since the woman could have been on time, she would now have to wait for next week's eye clinic.

Soon after that, John Mangadima, Helen's nursing student and friend, came to find her. He rebuked Helen for turning the woman away. "Couldn't you see that she was blind? She has waited all morning at the roadside for someone to lead her to the Christian doctor who heals people. She is a soul for whom Christ died—and you have harshly turned her away. Would Jesus have done so?" Helen regretted her action. She resolved to breathe a quick prayer whenever she answered the door— no matter what the time—that she could receive each visitor as Jesus would.

She knew that a missionary is sent by God to live a Christian life, usually among people unlike him or her. This may involve preaching, teaching or doctoring, but it always involves personal relationships, often lived out in hard circumstances. These relationships are at the heart of ministry, and she often felt she was blowing it. But how could she possibly slow down? What task could she leave out? Her personality loved to run full steam like a locomotive, to charge into all in her path. And whenever she undertook a task, she felt responsible to see it was done right.

Fortunately, the mission brought in Dr. John Harris to work with—and actually over—Helen. He supervised the hospital work while she developed the nursing school and jungle clinics. Even though the change was a great help to her, Helen

fought giving up total leadership and control. It was hard for her to pare down her
own vision to make room for the visions of
others; to allow her own gifts to meld with
the gifts of others. She felt lonely as she
grappled with this change.

One morning Helen was teaching a Bible
study from Philippians 3:1–11. On the
blackboard she drew a large red cross. To
one side of it she listed the things people
count as important in this life: popularity,
wealth, security, and so on. On the other
side of the cross she wrote only "To know
Him . . ." The Holy Spirit seemed to use what
Helen said to reach into the hearts of many
of the listening workers and students, helping them to see where they had sinned and
where their priorities were wrong. They
came up to Helen in tears, repenting for
sins and asking her to pray for them. Pressure boiled up in Helen. How could she be
used to bring others to renewal in such a
way when she *herself* felt so dry and cold?
She ran from the church to her house and
lay on the floor sobbing, asking God for
mercy.

Pastor Ndugu was passing through
Nebobongo that morning on his bicycle.
Hearing about the commotion in the
church, he came to Helen's house and sat
quietly on the floor beside her, listening as

she spewed out all her guilt and frustration. Then he told her to get her backpack and her bicycle, and they rode together the sixteen miles to Pastor Ndugu's village.

Helen often related to the Africans more easily than to her fellow missionaries, because her days were fully spent for and with the Africans. Pastor Ndugu was like a father to Helen, and she often spent weekends with his family.

Tamoma, the pastor's wife, prepared a room for Helen, and Pastor Ndugu firmly but kindly told her to get in it and get right with God. For three days Helen fasted and prayed. For some time the sky seemed like brass, her Bible readings cold and dry. If God didn't come to her, she figured, well . . . she would continue her work teaching the nurses. She would even continue to teach the Bible, which she did not doubt for a minute to be God's word to man. But she would no longer accept support money as a missionary.

On Sunday night, as villagers dispersed to their own homes around ten o'clock, Helen joined Pastor Ndugu and his wife around the embers of their fire outside their home. For a while they sat in silence, a silence you could feel. "Please, can't you help me?" she asked quietly.

Pastor Ndugu opened his Bible to Galatians 2:20 and read:

> *I have been crucified with Christ; and it
> is no longer I who live, but Christ lives in
> me, and the **life** which I now live in the
> flesh I live by faith in the Son of God, who
> loved me, and delivered Himself up for me.*

He drew a vertical line in the dirt with
his heel. "Helen," he said quietly after a
long pause, "the trouble with you is that
we can see so much Helen that we cannot
see Jesus. You're so caught up in your own
concerns, your vision, and your medical
program." Again he paused and her eyes
filled with tears. "I notice that you drink
much coffee," he continued. "When they
bring you a mug of hot coffee, you always
stand holding it, waiting for it to cool
enough to drink. May I suggest that every
time, as you stand and wait, you lift your
heart to God and pray, 'Please, God, cross
out the I.'" As he said this, he moved his
heel in the dirt across the center of the I to
make a cross— †.

Then, as they prayed together the Spirit
of God seemed to reach into Helen's heart,
breaking down the barriers there. He
seemed to turn on the faucet. Helen prayed,
first with slight drips, then a steady burst,
unburdening her heart of its pride and self-
ishness and stubbornness and fear and
sense of failure. It all poured out. Gently,
softly, Pastor Ndugu prayed with her point

by point, drawing her away from her sins to see Jesus on the cross taking them for her. He prayed with her about instances where she needed to ask someone's forgiveness or to make things right. Finally, a great calm swept over her, and she felt washed clean.

As Helen cycled back to Nebobongo on Monday morning, she was met by some students who had prayed for her and were happy to see a new light in her eyes.

Although Helen would find she had not so much won the battle as prepared for "round two," she drew on the strength the Lord gave her each day, and her prayers cooled her cups of coffee.

Now that Dr. Harris had taken over responsibility for the patients at Nebobongo, Helen turned her attention toward building a network of forty clinics in the outlying areas. One week she taught nurses and the children and helped out in the hospital and maternity wards. The following week she visited clinics, seeing up to 2,500 patients a week, preaching the gospel and training workers at each small clinic to use twelve basic medicines.

But as much as Helen loved this work, she was too tired to give it her all. After five years at this grueling pace, it was time for a break, time to go home for a longer rest. So Helen planned to take a furlough.

A new friend, a sixteen-year-old girl named Susan, helped get Helen through the last few months before furlough. Susan had been expelled from primary school for rebelliousness but had later come to faith in Jesus Christ and had come to Nebobongo to learn to be a midwife. Shortly after she arrived, she was found to have leprosy. Helen took the discouraged girl into her home while she received treatment. Helen said she could continue her classes sitting apart from the other students. These two needy women, so different yet so alike, spent golden time together each morning, studying the Bible and praying together over cups of coffee.

If anyone had told her then, Helen would not have believed that after a few months at home on furlough she would tell WEC she was not coming back.

5

CONGOLESE IN CHARGE

At home on the coast of Cornwall in England, for a month Helen cared for her sick mother, rested and walked on the craggy beach. This life would have been too quiet for Helen except that she was not well herself. She then spent a month in the Tropical Hospital for treatment of chronic amoebic dysentery and the removal of her appendix.

On the mend, Helen traveled around the British Isles for twelve weeks, speaking in churches about WEC's work in Africa, particularly about the revival in the Congolese church and in many individuals, including herself. She was an effective, popular speaker and couldn't help enjoying the attention she received after the struggle her life had been in the Belgian Congo.

Feeling back to full stride, Helen worked long hours in a London hospital helping stem the tide of an influenza epidemic. She received a regular pay check for the first time in her life and was able to buy things for her mother, take trips and send money to the Congo. In her mind, her work in Africa shifted to a different hue—fuzzier, darker. Life was not a struggle in England as it had been in Africa.

There was also a certain man in her life; and although he was a mature Christian, he had no interest in the mission field. Helen feared that if he knew she was committed to return to Africa, perhaps he wouldn't be interested in her.

She told herself, *Surely the Lord doesn't expect you to return to Africa without a mate. You deserve someone to look after you and be a companion. Face it: you're lonely.*

Helen quit the mission, permed her hair, bought some new clothes, and tried to win a husband.

Not that her friend really encouraged her. As much as she would have liked to read more into his manner and interest toward her, Helen could not say he honestly seemed interested in marriage.

However there was one Person who did continue very interested in Helen. She didn't want God's way in her life right now; she wanted to try a stint at the helm herself. But in the inner turmoil that gripped her, she realized as never before that Jesus Christ was not just *for* her, He lived *within* her. And He loved her enough to want to fight for her.

Eventually Helen realized the turmoil was not good. She and her friend agreed to quit seeing each other. She accepted the fact that by the grace of God—by His love for her though she did not deserve it—Christ was in her, and He wanted the best for her. Helen asked God again to accomplish His purpose through her: to repair more walls, if need be. She wrote to WEC, thanking them for a year's leave of absence and for their prayers and submitting her application to return to the Congo.

But the kaleidoscope of the Belgian Congo as Helen knew it had turned dramatically. She returned two weeks before the day the Belgians planned to grant the colony independence. Unfortunately, the Africans had been given very little preparation to assume roles of leadership. Whites were leaving the Belgian Congo at that time, and the Africans were celebrating their departure. No one knew what would happen next, what sort of instability, nor how the remaining whites would be treated.

When Helen's ship arrived at the port at Mombasa, Kenya, the immigration officers would not stamp her passport nor give her permission to disembark from the ship until she guaranteed someone (her father) would pay for her return fare to England.

Things *appeared* as usual. Africans waved and cheered as Helen passed through villages on her way to Nebobongo. But she sensed the urgent need to take a pulse on what was developing around her. Dr. Harris and his wife looked drawn and weary, and left on their own well-timed furlough now that Helen could take charge.

Helen listened carefully to everyone: nursing students, villagers who came for medical care, radio reports from the capital. The air was thick with rumors, threats, unrest and uncertainty.

One evening during Helen's first week back, the African male nurses met with elders of the church. They then summoned Helen and the only other three white people left in Nebobongo. The Africans were polite but quickly stated their purpose. "We want to appoint an African leader over the hospital," one said. "Everywhere else has done it. We want you to hand over authority to John Mangadima." The four whites hesitated, praying silently for wisdom.

John Mangadima spoke and broke the tension. "I don't mind being in charge of the nurses and the general administrative work. But I'm not a doctor and we can't do without our doctors, and I couldn't ever be over them." Helen and her companions let out their breaths. There was to be a definite change in authority, but they had not had to fight it. And it was obvious that the Africans wanted them to stay.

June 30, 1960, was Independence Day for the country, which was renamed Zaire. It was a day of prayer and celebration for Christians, with a soccer match in the afternoon. The headman from the closest village came with six other village headmen to visit the missionaries at Nebobongo. The men wore native straw hats with flowers, loincloths instead of the now-typical European way of dress, and carried a bouquet of flowers and some eggs. They invited their white "strangers" to stay with their people in their new independence.

But truckloads of soldiers also rumbled through Nebobongo, taunting the Europeans with songs in native languages, threatening harm to them upon their return. For the next four years, the young government grappled with how to rule the country, wealthy in resources but also poor in economy and diverse in tribes and languages. The medical work continued at Nebobongo, but in a country where Africans had just thrown off rule by whites, the white missionaries who remained could not feel very secure.

In early 1961 the government asked Helen to help them at the Wamba Hospital

sixty miles east of Nebobongo. She drove
to Wamba to operate and see patients twice
a week, leaving at 5:30 a.m. and returning
at 10:30 p.m. She set off on February 13th
as usual, with John Mangadima along to
help. Six miles from Wamba they were
stopped and warned to go home. "There is
great trouble in Wamba. All the whites are
being tied up. Go home." They argued that
as medical workers they couldn't. They had
a responsibility to their patients.

Helen encouraged John to let her go on
alone, not wanting to endanger him.
"Never!" he exclaimed. "If it is safe for you
to go, I go with you."

The road was barricaded just before
Wamba. Soldiers jeered at Helen and ordered her out of the car. "Do not touch her!"
John exclaimed. "She is our doctor, one of
us"—using a word in the local tongue
meaning "blood of our blood." They backed
away.

At the government office in town, they
were assured they could come and go
safely, but they also learned the reason for
the unrest. Patrice Lumumba, popular
leader of the rebel Simbas, had been murdered.

Returning home, they pulled off the road
at a junction where all three intersecting
roads were blocked off and khaki-clad sol-

diers were searching each car for whites. Helen and John settled in for a long, uneasy wait.

Suddenly, inexplicably, they were waved forward, the barriers were removed for them, and soldiers smartly saluted them as they sailed past. They never learned why.

Zaire was a bubbling cauldron of discontent which boiled over on August 7, 1964, when the regional capital of Stanleyville was captured by Simba, or "Lion," rebels. The country was thrown into anarchy. While the Protestant missionaries, who at Nebobongo now included only Helen and two other women, were allowed to continue their work, rebels began a reign of terror, brutally torturing and killing those who had been involved in the young government since independence.

Thieves stripped goods from homes and stores. Frightened villagers armed themselves with bows and arrows. Teenagers and sometimes even younger children were recruited by the Simbas as "Lion Cubs" and took the law into their own hands.

Cars and trucks were stolen by the rebels to haul their soldiers around. When a vehicle rumbled through Nebobongo, Helen's nerves went taut at either of the two likely possibilities: rebels had come to threaten them and steal valuables, or a wounded rebel was being brought for emergency treatment. The latter was as frightening to Helen as the former, because she had never been able to shake a dread of grisly wounds or of performing surgery. She feared she would not be able to give the help needed.

The Africans whom she treated looked up to her as their doctor who could work wonders. She often had no fellow doctor to consult with about difficult cases. The life-and-death decisions fell to her, and she trembled at the responsibility.

Actually, Helen became quite a good surgeon, but she never lost a crushing fear of operating. As she grew used to the feeling, however, she began to see beyond it and came to realize that the fear pushed her to be minute-by-minute in touch with God. And God gave her an amazing peace beyond understanding.

On a Friday evening, seventeen Lion Cubs wielding spears, lances, knives and screaming filthy language stormed into the Bible school where Helen was teaching. They demanded that Helen give them the car keys. The car was the missionaries' only way out of Nebobongo for food and medical equipment—and for escape, if necessary.

The car, a van, was no gem. It had no

lights or wipers (Helen had tampered with them so no one would try to steal the car at night). It burned oil furiously, needed the spark plugs cleaned every ten miles and had worn-out tires.

Helen requested that their leader step forward and stated that she could talk only with him. He swaggered forward, a small, wiry twelve-year-old dressed as a lieutenant. After an hour of haggling, Helen gave in to the upstart, insisting that she would back the car out of the garage. He wanted to drive but had never even sat in a car before. If he wanted to wreck the car and kill himself—fine. But she wanted to save her house and garage.

The Lieutenant's pride at being behind the wheel was dampened by the fact that his feet didn't reach the pedals. After ten minutes, frustrated and cursing, he let Helen drive. They set off with no lights, in dim moonlight, with a storm fast rising. All seventeen had stuffed themselves into the van—as well as two nurses who came along: Joel and John Mangadima. They pulled into a garage two miles away, where the Lion Cubs demanded oil and gas and forced the mechanic to work to repair the lights.

Helen stood in the dark in pouring rain, waiting silently for the mechanic to discover that she had tampered with the lights. Death felt very near. She became conscious that she was not alone. On either side of her in the shadows stood Joel and John.

As the engine roared to life, then died, the Lieutenant asked the mechanic if there had been foul play (Helen had also tampered with the starter). "Definitely," the mechanic replied. Helen, Joel and John were silhouetted in the headlights, and the seventeen youths, enraged, sprang toward them.

The three tensed to receive blows, but suddenly the youths' strides were checked as if in an odd game of freeze tag. The three felt as if an invisible barrier of glory surrounded them. The youths turned, seeming to have forgotten about them. Laughing and jeering, they piled into the van and forced the mechanic to drive them off into the stormy night. Before Helen, John and Joel had walked far along the muddy road toward home, a passing truck gave them a lift.

In the midst of such episodes, day-to-day life continued. There were babies to deliver and classes to teach—to the orphan children and to the nurses. Helen felt sorry for these young Africans for whom the future was so unsettled.

Cars and trucks bearing Simbas continued their visits to Nebobongo. At the end of a particularly trying day, Helen and a friend would play Scrabble to "cleanse their minds." But one particular night she would not forget—ever.

6

EVIL ON THE RAMPAGE

The uneasiness which invaded life on the mission station at Nebobongo thrived in the blackness of jungle night. Helen preferred to live alone, to have some privacy after the intensity of her days. But at times one or another of the nursing students or other female missionaries came to stay in the house with her.

The rebels, or Simba lions, warred against "traitors" who had sided with the government over the past four years. The rebels believed the government had stolen the country's wealth and misled her people. But there were no courts to decide who was "guilty" of these crimes. And the "guilty" were tortured and killed.

The northeast province where Nebobongo was located was so remote that it saw less fighting than many other areas. But still, undisciplined teenage Lion Cubs and Simbas took rule into their own hands from their local stronghold in Paulis.

Rumor said that 1,000 had been killed in Paulis. Bloodshed had occurred in the

streets and bodies were buried 50 at a time
in mass graves. In the area of Nebobongo,
local chiefs were beaten by rebels.

Roads were blocked and travelers ques-
tioned. The missionaries no longer received
mail from the outside world. Stealing was
rampant—especially automobiles. Each
day fleeing government soldiers sped by
with their wives and children in stolen cars
and trucks, sometimes in vehicles whose
owners Helen knew.

The mission station was safer than many
places for three reasons: Its buildings sat
back off the main road; it was several miles
from rebel headquarters; and few people
lived there. To date, Protestant whites had
been left alone to go about their business
because it was believed they hadn't been
involved in politics (policies of the past
government had favored Roman Catholics).
Besides, a medical hospital was important
for the rebels as well as for the other side.

Still, the station was subject to searches
and theft. Helen now hid one wheel, the
spare tire, the battery and the coil wire of
her car in her house.

Except for the periodic banging on the
doors by rebels wanting one thing or another, life took on an eerie quiet at
Nebobongo. There were very few patients
except in the maternity hospital. School

was canceled, partly so that children who walked to school from neighboring villages wouldn't be captured and forced to serve as Lion Cubs.

Helen still taught Bible classes, preparing study notes in Swahili. She now had the time the busy years had stolen from her to study the Word, and she seemed to move immersed in it. Somehow, living as she was in the rough and raw of life and close to nature, she sensed a new closeness to the Bible writers and their times. She moved within the peace God gave to her. She knew that at any time she could be killed and go to meet her Savior, and she wanted to be ready.

God had promised, "I will never leave thee nor forsake thee." His presence was very real to Helen.

Just after her midday meal one afternoon a carload of Lions rumbled up to Helen's house. "We have orders," said the officer, "to inspect your house and take any radios or tape recorders."

"I have none, but you're welcome to look," said Helen, who had been advised to cooperate with them however possible. It was an attitude which went against her natural reaction when faced with bullying and misconduct.

Every cupboard, every drawer, every

suitcase and trunk was turned inside out. They found nothing.

One of the "inspectors" was obviously ill, and Helen took him over to the hospital to get him some medicine. She even pleasantly offered him a carton of fresh fruit—oranges, mangoes and blackberries. The officer returned later that night to pick up the fruit. When Helen opened the car door for him so he could load his carton in, she saw on the floor and seats five or six tape recorders, a radio and a typewriter. She shut the car door and wished him good night. Then, with muttered comments, Helen returned to cleaning up her own possessions.

The amazing thing was that the two missionary women next door had two radios and two tape recorders, but no one seemed to ask for theirs. Helen and the two women discussed the situation. The radio, particularly, was a crucial source of news for them of what was happening in the capital and the outside world. They could hide the radios in a trunk and bury the trunk in the jungle. But if it was found, would they be shot for hiding them? Worse yet, would the Africans who helped hide them be beaten? And in the Lord's eyes, would hiding them be like lying?

They decided to place these treasures on

the table in full view and be done with the matter. They read the day's selection from the devotional *Daily Light*, which included the verse "Greater is He who is in you than he who is in the world." Then they prayed together and went to bed. Eventually a friend who happened to be in the Simba army took the radios and tape recorders away for safekeeping.

Pounding on the front door awakened Helen one night at about 1:00 a.m. "Open the door to the Armee Populaire or we will smash it in!"

Helen leaped out of bed, pulled on her bathrobe, reached for a kerosene lamp, and rushed to the door. She called to the two male student nurses who were staying in the house with her and they came, trembling.

Six armed rebels demanded to see her husband. When Helen said she had none, they accused her of hiding him. They scoured the house, rifling through drawers and stealing whatever took their fancy: her watch, money set out for buying food, berets, a record player and records. This part of the routine Helen had become used to.

They sent the two nurses to the car carrying their booty for them as Helen herded the bullies out the front door.

But the Lieutenant, with a hand on the pistol at his hip, crudely ordered Helen back into the house. Horrified, she turned and bolted around the house and into the darkness of the jungle in back. Flinging herself under bushes in oozing mud, she covered her head, hands and feet with her bathrobe to hide her white skin from any light. Huddled motionless except for her pounding heart, Helen prayed they would leave, as they had at other times, since they had gotten what they came for.

Their coarse laughter carried to her. They followed her with flashlights, shouting that she had hidden something from them and must be found. In a few minutes they did find her, yanked her up and pushed her back toward the house. One soldier, in an odd gesture of kindness, searched for her glasses in the mud, cleaned them off and handed them to her.

The Lieutenant shoved her and struck her on the head with a rubber club. On the verandah, Hugh, a nursing student, tried to stand in front of Helen to protect her, but he was mercilessly beaten.

The Lieutenant forced Helen back into the house at gun point, to her bedroom at the back, and ordered her to put on clean clothes. Then for a half hour he beat and assaulted her as she cried out to Jesus in pain and fear and shame and misery.

Finally, with his flashlight blinding her, he ordered her to get dressed and get into the car with him and the other Lions. They would take her to Ibambi. "Put on your best dress," the Lieutenant commanded. "Now you are my wife."

Pressed into the car with the soldiers, Helen sang choruses in Swahili with what strength she could muster. She sang to quiet her racing heart, and so that the Lions would hear over and over the name of Jesus and that the devil in them would fear and tremble. *"Greater is He who is in you than he who is in the world."* (1 John 4:4)

As the car neared the mission station at Ibambi, the Lieutenant asked Helen how many Americans were there. When she hesitated to answer, he struck her again. But they didn't stop at the mission. They drove into the center of town. Helen was led into a house and thrown into a bedroom, where she crept to the chair in the corner and—left alone—tried to calm her aching heart. Scripture verses flowed into her mind, and she pleaded that the Lord would give her strength and faith. Her own were quite used up.

Near dawn other prisoners were put in the room with her: five Roman Catholic nuns, three priests and a lay worker, then four Greek businessmen. They stole glances at one another, afraid to talk. Then, cautiously, smiles passed around—Helen's through swollen eyes and lips.

The Lions said they had been given instructions by radio to speedily round up all aliens (whites). The group in the room continued to grow. More nuns and priests were brought, then her fellow missionaries from the station at Ibambi, her two neighbor women from Nebobongo, and a Belgian couple from a plantation.

Helen asked and received permission to cross the road to the home of one of the Greek men. A Simba guard followed her, but didn't disturb her as the Greek's wife helped her wash up as best she could, and Helen unburdened her aching heart to her. The Greek woman, now a captive and thousands of miles from her children in Cyprus, was glad to have a woman to talk to as well. The Greek couple served all the prisoners and Lions coffee, bread and cheese.

By about 9:30 a.m. they were again on the move, this time squashed together in the back of a truck under the glare of the tropical sun. As uncomfortable as was the ride, the breeze on Helen's face and the pack of friends surrounding her were a balm after the loneliness and panic of the night. She began singing and chatting with her companions, until a woman looked over at her in amazement. "My, you'll still be talking when they shoot you!" she laughed.

The prisoners reached rebel headquarters at Paulis just as the 2:00 p.m. bugle sounded. They were unloaded and separated into three groups in the welcome shade of the jacaranda trees: Roman Catholic nuns, priests and Belgians, and the Protestants.

But the rebels at Paulis were mystified; the Commander was furious. Who gave these orders? Why were they here? "Put them back in the truck and take them all home!"

It was a slow trip home. The driver and their rebel escorts were saturated with beer —perhaps to choke their embarrassment. As drenching rain began, a tarp was pulled over the back of the truck. It was then muggy in the back, and hot and thick with cigarette smoke. But along the route Africans waved and cheered to see the prisoners were being brought home.

At Nebobongo, after hugs and singing by the Africans, Helen hastily packed a suitcase and she and her neighbors rode on with their fellow missionaries to Ibambi. At Ibambi, Pastor Ndugu hovered over her and took her with him to the home of Jack and Jessie Scholes, her missionary leaders, for supper, Bible reading and prayer. Exhausted and sore, Helen entered a fitful sleep, with dreams of cars arriving. For the present, until she recovered and probably until the war was settled, all the missionaries would stay together at Ibambi.

In the following days the conflict seemed to reach a climax, as the missionaries listened by radio. On November 3rd after dinner at 1:00 p.m., they tuned in to the pageantry of the opening of Parliament, broadcast from London. The Queen had just started her speech. The missionaries—most of them British—stood for the playing of the British national anthem. Teary eyed, they were feeling very loyal and very homesick when at 2:00 p.m. Lions drove up and went straight to the garage to try to steal the cars. They couldn't get the cars to run, but the moment was spoiled, as the missionaries had to put the radio away.

Government troops advanced toward Stanleyville to recapture the capital. With only 100 miles to go, they appealed to the Lions to lay down their arms, turn in their leaders and protect all foreigners.

But Lion leaders retaliated, declaring that all whites were prisoners of war and that violence would be met with violence. The local Lion leaders, not willing to give up their stranglehold on the province until necessary, warned the missionaries at Ibambi to each have one suitcase and a briefcase packed and ready at any moment to be "relocated."

7

FINAL CAPTURE

John Mangadima, in charge of the medical center at Nebobongo but with no doctors left there, worked under great pressure. The station was infested with Lions. Some were patients in the wards. Others followed the nurses as they tried to make rounds. John couldn't unlock the door of the pharmacy storeroom without a following of thugs who tried to help themselves from the shelves. He had to show great diplomacy, courage and wisdom—and he did.

John had little hope now of receiving any supplies. If the medical work was to continue, he knew he must conserve the medicines carefully and certainly not permit them to be stolen.

One midnight John slipped into the pharmacy storeroom and quietly went to work. He divided everything into ten piles: the penicillin and aspirin was all divided, as were the anti-malarial drugs, the vitamins, the thermometers and bandages, the needles and syringes, the powders and creams. He packaged each of the ten piles into plastic bags in ten separate boxes and labeled the contents.

Slipping out the storeroom door, John stole to the home of a trusted village workman and roused him as quietly as possible. "Go out right now, in the dark," John whispered, "and bury this box somewhere. Don't look inside, so if asked about it later you won't know the contents. One day I'll ask you for it, but until then hide the box and forget about it!"

Through the early morning hours John took each of the ten boxes to a different village workman, giving identical instructions.

Over the course of the next few months, every six weeks or so John visited another workman and asked for his box. The supplies never ran out, and the work of the medical center at Nebobongo continued.

Meanwhile, Helen spent her days quietly at Ibambi, waiting . . . and also making sense of what had happened to her. She had a profound awareness that as Jesus Christ lived within her, His purity was hers, and she need suffer no shame. She found priceless treasure, too, in having known the fellowship of His suffering—what it was like for Christ to suffer on the cross when He had done nothing wrong. These verses were precious to her:

*For what credit is there if, when you sin
and are harshly treated, you endure it with
patience? But if when you do what is right
and suffer for it you patiently endure it, this
finds favor with God. For you have been
called for this purpose, since Christ also
suffered for you, leaving you an example
for you to follow in His steps, who committed no sin . . .* (1 Peter 2:20–22a).

Well aware of her many fears and inse-
curities, Helen often thought of a phrase
which encouraged her, from her WEC
friend Norman Grubb: "A courageous man
is not one who does not know fear, but one
who, knowing fear, overcomes it."

When would it all be over? At Ibambi the
missionaries prayed for rescue, for the protection of the other whites remaining in
Zaire and for the peace of their loved ones
back home.

The final banging on the door came on
November 24th. The missionaries were told
to come to the truck outside, each bringing a suitcase, a briefcase, a cushion and
a blanket. Piled in the back of the truck
were twenty-four African men, four African women, all their baggage, two goats,
chickens, a drum of palm fat, huge
bunches of bananas, and the seven missionaries with their gear. Helen was
perched high on the trunks and suitcases,
with her heels on Jessie Scholes' shoul-

ders, hanging on to a Lion for dear life at
every swing and lurch of the truck.

The truck made continual stops to buy
food or for the Lions to greet friends along
the road. Hoping that at any minute the
government army would overtake and rescue them, the missionaries had a large
Union Jack, the British flag, hidden in their
luggage. One Lion in the back of the truck
carried a hand grenade to throw at any
approaching jeep.

Their destination proved to be the Roman Catholic convent at Wamba, where
they arrived soon after dark. The two missionary men, Brian Cripps and Jack
Scholes, were sent to the priests' quarters.
The five women were graciously welcomed
by the Mother Superior to join 45 nuns,
two Belgian women and their five children.

As the Mother Superior showed the
women into the tiny room they would
share, she drew the door partly shut and
whispered, "Be careful. You will be
watched." Then, opening the door to exit,
she raised her voice: "Supper will be served
whenever you're ready."

They had been told by the Commander
that their luggage would be inspected in
the morning, which raised the problem of
the large Union Jack. The Lions would
know this wasn't their flag, and there would

be trouble. So after supper the women took turns cutting the flag into tiny strips with fingernail scissors, pausing any time guards seemed to be walking by the door so no one would hear the scissors squeak. They then stuffed the strips into a cushion and resewed the cushion's seams.

The Commander, who was himself a Roman Catholic, seemed genuinely concerned for the welfare of his captives and interested in protecting them. When he was around, they fared well.

But the other Lions behaved in the manner the missionaries were more used to. They were abusive toward some of the young nuns. And at night the women sometimes heard gunshots and commotion from the priests' quarters. They feared for Brian Cripps and Jack Scholes, and were always relieved when after a period of days had passed they were allowed to see them. In one case Brian had been beaten on the head and back. The Catholic priests generally fared worse. The husbands of the two Belgian women with children had been murdered, but the women had not seen the bodies and could not allow themselves to believe it was true.

There were few outlets for Helen's abundant energy. She organized the women into teams to assist the nuns with the daily chores, and read from the library of French books housed at the convent.

She found the Mother Superior quite remarkable. She was always composed and gracious, despite the Lions' constant demands. And every time the doorbell rang, whereas the other women cowered inside, waiting and praying, the Mother Superior answered and dealt with each situation.

Surely we'll be rescued by Christmas, Helen thought as the days passed. The government army must be near by now. Surely our worried families at home will have word from us by Christmas.

But Christmas came, and they planned the best celebration they could. The two turkeys were killed and cooked, and cakes and jellies were made by Jessie Scholes. Helen—never a good helper in the kitchen —typed out carols which they all sang: "Silent Night" in Swahili and "O Come All Ye Faithful" in French. The nuns sang a special Christmas mass.

Then a change came on December 28th. They were hurriedly packed up and driven in shifts to an isolated roadhouse. Although their guards continued to feed them, they now also had to protect them. Hostile Lions and Lion Cubs broke the windows and taunted them with spears and clubs, wanting to kill the whites. The prisoners slept on the floor behind the largest pieces of furniture for protection. They were told they would be moved on, but two cramped, tense days passed. The guards quarreled almost continually with the local Lions who wanted the whites' blood.

Early in the morning of December 30th, the guard was changed, to the prisoners' dismay. Their guards had generally been good to them, but this new bunch looked suspect. At 7:30 a.m., planes droned overhead, and the prisoners were herded to the middle of the room. "If we are killed," the guards said, "you will be too." They heard distant bombing.

The guards thought one of them must have contacted the planes somehow and demanded to know who had a "transmitter," searching their luggage.

Missionary Nurse Florence Stebbing had her hearing aid in her suitcase. She took it to them, knowing that if they found it in her suitcase, there would be trouble. They were sure that it was the transmitter, not understanding her explanation of what it was. They fired questions at Florence and struck her.

The guards continued looking through the luggage—the Belgians had much more so theirs took more time. Then they told their captives they would be shot immediately. Lions were gathering outside the house with every sort of weapon.

Suddenly machine gun fire was heard approaching the house and all dropped to the floor for cover. Their rescuers, twenty-five soldiers, burst through the door. It was over.

That night the whites were safe at the government army headquarters in Paulis, joining other refugees. They stretched out for the night on clean mattresses, having had baths and a large supper, at which they all tearfully sang the doxology. This was better than the best party, the grandest celebration Helen had ever known. With her whole heart Helen praised God for His goodness and faithfulness.

The missionaries were sped through the formalities of leaving the country. Their joy was tempered with sorrow when they heard about friends who had not survived. But by midnight on New Year's Day 1965, Helen was en route to London. She was happy to have her life and liberty; but her heart ached, too, for the Africans she had left behind at Nebobongo.

8

"YOU BUILD; I'LL TEACH"

After a year in England, Helen heard that
the government army was firmly in
control of the northeast province of Zaire.
Two senior missionaries from WEC returned to "spy out the land" and said that
it was safe for women as well as men to
return.

In deciding whether to go back, Helen
had to relive the terror of the last awful
months of 1964 and get past it. Could she
take such a risk again? It would no doubt
take many years for Zaire to become po-
litically stable, with so much of the country in ruins and its people in poverty.

Helen also had to look back over her
eleven years in Africa and the part God had
enabled her to play. Was her role logically
finished, or did God have a part for her in
the mammoth job of rebuilding?

Exactly what the task might involve was
practically impossible to imagine from the
comfort of an English home. Greek trad-
ers in Zaire reported that everything was

destroyed: buildings, equipment, schools, hospital supplies. Were they exaggerating?

And were the white missionaries really wanted back? For fifty years the Congolese had had to show patience and deference to their white rulers. Now there was an understandable national distrust of foreigners. Perhaps the Africans wanted to try to go it alone. While Helen had had a year's rest, the Africans had been living in misery. Would they resent her authority over them and care nothing about her plans and dreams?

Then the letters came from Africa, pleading that she come. John Mangadima wrote that the shelves in the pharmacy were nearly empty. Each day at the hospital saw endless lines of patients. An African medical team of five continued the work at Nebobongo, and another four were at outlying clinics. But they worked out of love for their people because there were no more funds for salaries. Eleven of the 48 nursing students in school when the war broke out wanted John to teach them "until our doctor returns." He ended his letter: "We don't really expect you to come back after all you suffered for our people, but if God should persuade you to, we will never cease to thank Him, and to love you and care for you as never before."

It was the desire of Helen's heart to go, and the letters clinched it. On Easter morning 1966, Helen drove into Nebobongo. Word buzzed through the church, "They're here. They're here." Christians poured out of the church, hundreds and hundreds of them in a sea of joyful dancing and singing, praising God and hugging Helen till she felt all squeezed out. She was swept into the church, which was still standing though pockmarked from machine-gun fire.

Helen saw that the people were terribly thin. They had reverted to native dress of beaten-bark loincloths and grass skirts because they had no other clothing.

The following day Helen pulled up to the hospital in a new Land Rover. Christians had donated and fully equipped it as a mobile hospital unit. An amazed crowd gathered for a grand show-and-tell. Helen pulled out the rolled canvas stretcher on wheels, the stock of medicines, and the cupboard fitted with a microscope.

Then she made rounds among patients in the hospital. With dismay, she saw that the medicines she had brought with her would be just a drop in the bucket. She found patients thin as rakes, with tuberculosis coughs, skin diseases, eye diseases, tumors—you name it. But Helen set her energies to the task of treating patients and of gathering supplies from relief organizations and from neighboring countries.

In the midst of such need, each returning missionary had to assess his or her priorities. Although Helen's heart was with the people in Nebobongo, her vision took her elsewhere. Her burning desire remained constant: to train medical workers who could give both Christ's love and excellent care to their own people. She wanted to train Africans to care for their own people, no matter what the future.

Her dream now took her to Dr. Carl Becker, an American surgeon and missionary at the station of Nyankunde, 350 treacherous miles from Nebobongo. Dr. Becker was developing a large medical center at Nyankunde, built from the pooled resources of five missions and churches. The medical center would serve the Africans in a 500-square-mile region with five million people, in the great basin of a tropical rain forest.

The plan included a 250-bed hospital with the capacity to treat 1,000 outpatients per day. Helen's role would be to develop a training school there for nurse practitioners who would be trained and serve very much like doctors. Twenty-four new students would be accepted each year for a course that would last three years. The school would develop better there than at the small hospital in Nebobongo. After two days of meetings and prayer, the church leaders at Ibambi reluctantly released Helen for this new task and wished her God's blessing.

Soon after her move to Nyankunde, early one morning Helen stood on the verandah of her temporary home. Across the valley the hills were still wrapped in mist. Nestled in the valley below were fields and gardens and the sprawling hospital buildings. The air was filled with the song of birds and the fragrance of frangipani flowers. Just below Helen, stretching up the hillside, was a field of four or five acres which would be the site of the nursing school and dormitories. She strode out over the ground and returned with an inch-thick layer of red mud on her sandals. She had only her dream now, but Helen rose to the challenge.

She sent word all over Zaire by radio and "bush telegraph" that any interested students should come to Nyankunde during the first week of August. And they came. During that week twenty-four students arrived in groups of four or five from different areas, with more to come in the weeks that followed. In all, they represented nine different tribes.

On the morning of registration, Helen sat on a wooden chair at a camp table set up in the driveway behind Dr. Becker's house. She took down the students' names and welcomed them. With John Mangadima—once more her assistant—she gave them each a blanket, plate, mug, spoon, lamp, bowl, matches and soap.

In front of them spread the steeply sloping field in the bowl of the hills, covered with thorn bushes and shoulder-high grasses, which was to become the school. When Helen looked up, she noticed the students' eyes straying across the valley, searching for the school and dormitories. Manasse, a tall African in sunglasses, stepped forward. "Where is the school, Doctor?" he asked.

With as cool a wave of the arm as Helen could manage, she pointed to the field and rising hillsides: "Over there." The students' eyes followed her.

"And the dormitories?"

"Also there." They began to understand as Helen assigned each student temporary lodging with church elders and missionaries.

Could Helen win the cooperation of these proud young men, so aware of their potential? They were some of the few Zairians

with high school educations. Each was
eager to assert his independence and enjoy the status of a job as a nurse practitioner. Few teenagers had survived the rebel-
lion in Zaire. These were the lucky ones,
and they were reaching for opportunity.

That afternoon Helen tramped the
ground with the students. She stood with
them, coated with burrs and mud, and
asked the question: "Are you willing to take
your shirts off and turn this valley into a
school and housing by sheer hard work? If
you will, I will teach you all I know. If you'll
build, I'll teach. Meet me in the courtyard
at 6:30 a.m. tomorrow and give me your
answer." About all Helen had in her favor
was that they had all journeyed some dis-
tance to get there, and for such training
they had nowhere else to go.

It was gray and drizzling at 6:30 when
Helen erected a crude shelter and sat down
to wait, reading her Bible. As time dragged
on, she read a portion, then a chapter, then
a book. She was chilled and soaked
through. Finally, at 8:45 a.m., they strag-
gled up to her, and she had won. She didn't
know where they had met or who had been
their leader, but obviously they had decided to take the challenge. They sang a
hymn together. Helen gave a brief Bible
study and assigned tasks. She divided the

students into three groups, each group with a set of tools, an appointed leader, and a job to do. The group with axes was to fell trees. The one with hoes would clear a dormitory site. Those with the knife-like scythes would mow down jungle grass for a soccer field and gardens.

They began without much enthusiasm, and it quickly became apparent that some of them had never used the tools before. But finally one laughed and said, "Okay, you win. We build and you teach!" And with the laughter the tension was broken.

Helen awarded prizes to the group which finished a task first. It wasn't easy to keep the students at hard work from 6:30 a.m. to 5:30 p.m. each day. But they began to pull together and to realize they really could do it. Their aim was to finish by October 1st so classes could begin.

The rainy season and illnesses delayed them. But on October 29th, the school opened with housing reasonably completed for the students and with classes held in borrowed public school rooms. In a semi-circle around the flagpole stood thirty-six male students in blue shirts with the school badge sewn on their pockets and three girls in blue and white pin-striped dresses. Dr. Becker prayed. Someone blew heartily on an old trumpet. John Mangadima unfurled the new Zairian flag, and the students stood smartly at attention for their national anthem. Then the men changed into tee-shirts to spend the afternoon at soccer.

It was now Helen's turn to teach and her old fears crept in. Was her knowledge up to today's teaching standards? Could she prepare these students adequately for the demands that would be made of them?

With an administrator and two other teachers, she began. Her days started with coffee at 5:00 a.m. and often ended after midnight. She taught classes, attended staff meetings, graded papers and prepared the next day's lesson—in French. On the 10-day semester break, Helen and a fellow teacher helped at the hospital in Nebobongo. Over Easter break, she helped workmen finish construction of her house. The pace suited her.

The staff and students worked hard and morale was high. An excellent start was made in the nurse practitioner and midwife training school at Nyankunde. But one problem would remain for the next seven years.

The graduating students could step into good jobs in mission or Red Cross hospitals. But for the students to get the best-paying jobs at government hospitals, the school had to have government accreditation. The students' diplomas had to bear a government signature and seal. And for this coveted status many things were required: permanent classrooms of a certain size with proper equipment, a library, a permanent dining hall, and endless paperwork. The forms were constantly changed and required numerous, hard-to-obtain signatures. Often government inspectors didn't show up, or those who did were not heard from again.

The process took more and more of Helen's time and attention over the following seven years. And the lack of government accreditation bred student unrest. Proud of their young country, the students were much quicker to blame the delay on white teachers than on government bungling and red tape.

In 1973, after Helen had spent a total of twenty years in Zaire, the desired government recognition was granted. But as Helen breathed "Thank you, God," with the proof in her hands, she was totally exhausted.

The students had staged a mass protest about how their new scholarship money from the government would be spent. They wanted the money in their own pockets. Helen was determined to spend most of it to run the school. Her view was overruled by the school administrative council, who compromised with the students. She was deeply hurt at what she saw as the students' rejection of her. She loved each student and had invested great time and energy for their welfare.

Yet through her pain she could still look at the situation objectively. Although it hurt, she sensed the Lord saying to her, "You no longer want Jesus only, but Jesus plus—plus respect, popularity, public opinion, success, pride. You want to finish in Zaire with all the trumpets blaring. You want a farewell that you organize for yourself, with photographs and tape-recordings to show and play at home, just to reveal what you have achieved. You want to feel needed and respected. You want the other missionaries to be worried about how they will ever carry on after you've gone. You'd like letters when you get home to tell you how much they realize they owe to you, how much they miss you. All this and more. Jesus *plus*. . . . No, you can't have it. Either it must be 'Jesus only' or you'll find you've no Jesus. You'll substitute Helen Roseveare."

After several days of inner silence Helen responded to the God she knew loved her, *Yes, Lord. I want Jesus only.*

In many ways, Helen *could* leave with the satisfaction of a job well done. She had seen fulfilled her vision of Africans trained to treat fellow Africans and to touch them with the love of Jesus Christ. She also knew that others would continue the work. Six weeks before Helen planned to leave Zaire, in August of 1973, Philip and Nancy Wood, both capable doctors, arrived to assume direction of the school. Helen liked them both very much and saw in them young people who could enjoy successful careers elsewhere but had chosen to serve the Lord at the medical center in Zaire.

Helen wanted to show them all she could of the medical work before she left. In truth, perhaps, she also wanted this last trip for herself. So Helen, Philip, Nancy, Basuana, their African driver, and several other Africans climbed in a mission van and headed for Nebobongo, 350 miles away, in the rainy season. The outing went smoothly until dusk on the first day of their return journey to Nyankunde. As their truck turned a corner and started to descend a hill, they saw a truck, no, two trucks, three, five—many trucks hugging the wooded sides of the road. At the bottom of the hill, surrounded by shouting truck drivers, was a twelve-ton truck sunk in an ocean of mud. They parked the van behind the other trucks and walked down the hill.

The swimming truck was loaded with over a hundred excited, snorting pigs, who to their delight had to be unloaded into the mud so the truck could be hauled out. While the pigs cavorted, the truck was shoved, heaved and pulled out of the mud. Then the shouting truck drivers herded the reluctant pigs back into captivity.

At about midnight, with that truck successfully on its way, the mission van was to go next. According to an unwritten trucker's law of the jungle, the smallest vehicle goes first. To lighten the load, all the passengers walked along the wooded embankment while Basuana drove the van through the mud with Helen beside him for moral support. Truckers walked through the mud ahead of the van in two lines. They showed where the firm ridges were, eighteen inches below the surface, that the van tires should drive on. Between this "safe ground" were pits of mud, in some places two or three feet deep.

Suddenly the van slid. Truckers grabbed for the van, but it turned on its side, and mud was slowly sucked into it.

Helen and Basuana were pulled from the cab, and waded, pulling their legs with great effort out of waist-deep mud. Helen was exhausted and shaken. She and Nancy walked up the hill to a nearby village to clean up, rest and wait, leaving the men to rescue the van.

At about 3:00 a.m. they heard the van and ran to the roadside to meet it. Philip, triumphant and smiling, was caked with mud from head to toe. Helen, feeling responsible, quickly apologized for leaving him with the van. After all, she was the one experienced with the language and customs and in getting truck drivers to help. "Come on, cut it out!" Philip protested. "This has been the most exciting night of my life!"

When Helen surveyed the valley and the school buildings hugging the hillsides of Nyankunde for a final time before she left Africa, she knew that she left the school in the hands of doctors with their own dreams. She watched with a chuckle as John Mangadima, now the medical director for his church area, took off on his new motorcycle up the gravel road for Ibambi as if he'd ridden one all his life. And she could see far off, in her mind's eye, the forty graduate nurse practitioners who were working in twenty-two hospitals in all parts of Zaire. Together they treated perhaps 3,000 patients a day with the healing combination of expert care and the good news of Jesus Christ.

At the school the Africans gave her a going-away party. So many friends attended: church elders and gardeners, tailors and plumbers. Her students served the steaming meal, Philip delivered his first speech in Swahili, and for two hours the guests recounted favorite stories about Helen. These were memories to carry with her.

The nurse practitioner training school was finally government-sanctioned and growing. Helen must find new walls to build.

9

A NEW VISION

Helen returned to London, where she cared for her aging mother. Then Helen herself had surgery for breast cancer. Thoughts of a return to Africa lessened, but not because of these troubles. Rather, an array of new people—hundreds, thousands, eventually over a million—were becoming Helen's new mission field. WEC asked Helen to travel all over the world, speaking to people about Jesus Christ and the need for Christians to care about others enough to share the gospel.

Helen was a wiry, straight-backed little lady with glasses and gray, salon-set hair. One day she stood on the platform of the train station in Belfast, Ireland. From the sky came not the usual soft drizzle, but torrents of rain. Shielded by her umbrella, Helen waited for her train.

A middle-aged woman joined her, thankful for Helen's invitation to share her umbrella since she lacked one of her own. The old shyness swept over Helen. She breathed a prayer: "Please, Lord, how can

I start a conversation?"

Across the tracks a huge billboard bore an ad for cigarettes. "That makes me mad," Helen said, in her direct way. The woman bristled at Helen's side. The British don't speak to strangers until properly intro- duced.

"You see," Helen continued, "I am a doc- tor. That sign makes young people want to smoke. Smoking causes lung cancer. Lung cancer causes death." Helen glanced at her umbrella-mate to see if she would speak. Instead, the woman began to weep.

The train pulled in, and Helen helped the woman onto the train and sat beside her. "May I help you?" Helen asked quietly.

"I've just come from City Hospital," the woman said, wiping her eyes with her handkerchief and blowing her nose. "They've told me I am dying of lung cancer because I have smoked all of my life. And," she continued with a sigh, "I don't know where I'm going after I die."

Helen rummaged in her purse and drew out her pocket-size Bible. From the Bible she drew a miniature copy of the *Wordless Book* with which she was adept at sharing the gospel, whether to a Zairian patient or, now, a frightened upper-middle-class Irish housewife. Helen blushed, aware that all those in the train compartment were listening. More importantly, she was thrilled to know she could help this woman become certain that she would spend eternity with God.

Whenever Helen wasn't traveling, she continued faithful to a particular commitment. Every Sunday afternoon she led a Bible study among a handful of teenage girls with the Girl Crusaders' Union (GCU). She had first led a GCU Bible study as a medical student. While Helen served in Africa, a GCU Bible study group had prayed for her; they were the ones who sent the precious package that held a hot-water bottle and a doll.

One Sunday afternoon Helen asked one of the girls to read 2 Timothy 1:6, "I put thee in remembrance that thou stir up the gift of God, which is in thee. . . ."

Helen told the girls this story from Nyankunde: The first permanent classroom building was nearing completion, and she was overseeing the finishing touches before the formal dedication ceremony.

The celebration had to be moved forward three weeks, leaving a ton of work for the week remaining. Helen rallied the students and workers to double their pace. Local carpenters produced chairs as fast as they could. As soon as these arrived, in batches of ten, some students sandpapered them and others varnished them, praying that the varnish would be dry before the board members sat on them.

Two students claimed they knew how to paint, so Helen dispatched them with two brushes and a one-gallon can of white, high-gloss paint to coat the window, door and blackboard frames in each schoolroom.

Moving from room to room to inspect the work, Helen searched for the painters. They were not in the first classroom, which surprised her. Nor were they in the second. Although the woodwork around the classroom remained brown, Helen touched one door gingerly, finding a sort of brown, sticky goo. She darted across to the library, where the painters were talking away, brushes in and out of the paint can, up and down the woodwork, totally unconscious that they were making no change in the color. The window frames looked just as before.

She peered into the paint can to find a solid mass of white, under a very thin layer of rapidly disappearing linseed oil. The paint had not been stirred!

There was no point in being annoyed. Helen reasoned that it was her fault for sending them off without instructions. Still, she was frustrated. They had waited months for the delivery of twelve cans of paint. By the time the paint arrived, three cans had already been stolen. Now another had been wasted. Helen marched off to fetch another can of paint.

With this one, she demonstrated the art of stirring. You had to stir clear through to the bottom of the can, and keep stirring the paint until the harder, colored layer was completely mixed into the oily layer on top. It then was of one consistency and color. It was ready to perform its task of covering wood with a fresh white.

Helen left the two students painting away. A half hour later, she remembered that she hadn't explained that the paint must be stirred every so often until the job was completed. She hurried back to the two boys, only to find that, sure enough, the paint and oil were separating and the paint was losing its whiteness. She stirred, explained, and left them to carry on.

Helen looked around at her Bible study girls, who listened intently. "We as Christians need to let God stir us, right down to the bottom of our innermost beings," she said. "We need to be stirred until there is no separation left between solid and liquid, between secular and spiritual, weekdays and Sundays. Our lives need to be of one consistency, through and through, ready to do the task for which we were cre-

ated. This stirring will need to be continued daily until that task is completed.

"One day on a hillside in England, I asked
God to stir me to serve Him, no matter if it
hurt. It's still the prayer of my heart. Now
I no longer need to prove God is worthy of
my life. And I no longer have to prove that
I'm able to serve Him. I simply want Christ
to live through me. . . . To 'cross' my I's. To
love people through me. To speak to them
about Christ through me. To care about
the world, through me."

The four girls sat, quiet and thoughtful,
and Helen led them in a closing prayer.
Then she watched as they gathered their
Bibles and notebooks and left, chattering
to one another. A seventeen-year-old,
Heather, stopped and turned on her way
out. "Oh, Dr. Roseveare, I've applied to
enter the university as a medical student.
Pray for me, won't you?" She smiled,
turned, joined her friends and moved on.

BIBLIOGRAPHY

Burgess, Alan, *Daylight Must Come.* New York: Delacorte Press, 1974.

"Helen Roseveare Motivation for Missions," videotape of message presented at Urbana '87, Inter-Varsity Christian Fellowship of the U.S.A., 1987.

"Mama Luka Comes Home," videotape, Vision Video, Worcester, PA.

Roseveare, Helen, *Doctor Among Congo Rebels.* Fort Washington, PA: CLC, 1965.

Roseveare, Helen, *Give Me This Mountain & He Gave Us a Valley.* Fort Washington, PA: WEC International, 1966.

Roseveare, Helen, *Living Faith.* Minneapolis, MN: Bethany House Publishers, 1980.

Roseveare, Helen, *Living Holiness.* Minneapolis, MN: Bethany House Publishers, 1986.

Roseveare, Helen, *On Track.* London: The Girl Crusaders' Union, 1990.

The hymn stanza on page 35 is from "Living Faith," by Mrs. A. Head. The quote is from Helen Roseveare's book *Living Faith* (Minneapolis, MN: Bethany House Publishers, 1980), page 10.